My
Unflappable
Mom

My Unflappable Mom

An Appreciation *of* Mothers

Images by Jonathan Chester

Words by Patrick Regan

Andrews McMeel Publishing, LLC

Kansas City · Sydney · London

Andrews McMeel Publishing, LLC
an Andrews McMeel Universal company
1130 Walnut Street, Kansas City, Missouri 64106

www.andrewsmcmeel.com

13 14 15 16 17 SDB 10 9 8 7 6 5 4 3 2 1

ISBN: 978-1-4494-2177-9

Library of Congress Control Number: 2012911289

ATTENTION: SCHOOLS AND BUSINESSES
Andrews McMeel books are available at quantity
discounts with bulk purchase for educational, business,
or sales promotional use. For information, please
e-mail the Andrews McMeel Publishing Special Sales
Department: specialsales@amuniversal.com

Introduction

*"Making the decision to have a child—it's momentous.
It is to decide forever to have your heart go walking around
outside your body."* —Elizabeth Stone

It's the world's hardest job, with the worst pay, and benefits that won't show up on any spreadsheet. It's twenty-four hours a day, every day, and each rising sun brings a new set of hurdles and hassles that only get replaced with tougher ones as the years go by.

It's motherhood, and it's no place for sissies.

Those with a basic knowledge of biology know that it's pretty simple to become a mother (though the final push is no picnic), but becoming a good mom is anything but easy. Becoming a great one is harder still. And becoming one of the best? Well, that's an honor reserved for a select few . . . like you, the amazing and exalted, the most rare of birds—the incredible, unflappable mom.

Moms are fluent in many languages.

The babblings of a baby, the ramblings of a toddler, the body language of adolescents, and the foreign tongue spoken by teenagers—the best moms can decipher them all.

Master the fine art of simply being there.

Words do not always need to be said. Grand gestures are rarely required. A parent who is present, emotionally and physically, is a gift. Period.

There's one on every block.

The fun mom. The expert blanket-fort builder. The lemonade-stand organizer. The mom all the neighbor kids love. The one who was never too busy to play—or at least made us feel that way. That's the mom I was lucky enough to have.

The Incredible Invisible Mom

To the casual observer, it might sometimes appear that moms are invisible to their offspring. For all the effect her words have, one might even assume that a mother speaks at a frequency inaudible to her children. Why is it that when you want their attention, you don't exist, but when you need a little quiet, they won't leave you alone?

Nobody's Fool

Every mom should wear a button that reads, "Don't even try." Don't even try to lie about who tracked in the mud, who flattened the just-about-to-bloom daffodils with a soccer ball, or who started the fight that led to the three-day suspension. Veteran moms aren't just unflappable—they're unfoolable. As Spanky from *Our Gang* memorably said, "You can fool some of the people some of the time, but you can't fool Mom."

Accept all, find beauty in each.

Every kid is gifted—some physically, some intellectually, and some in ways not as quick to emerge or as easy to categorize. Wise moms know the fundamental truth—there's pure beauty at the heart of every child.

Take the long view.

From the adolescent point of view, every pimple is Vesuvius. Every setback is the strikeout that loses the World Series. Every rejection is a rejection from the universe itself. Moms know better. Experience equals perspective. Bad day today? Guess what? A new one starts tomorrow.

Under the wing is a tricky thing.

There's a fine line between gentle guidance and overbearing oppression. The best moms instinctively know when to shelter and when to back off.

"Mother" spoken here.

Conversations between moms often begin like this: "You'll never guess what that little (expletive) has done this time. . . ." Moms have a language all their own, rife with terms of endearment, terms of frustration, and—akin to that old (apocryphal) saying about Eskimos and snow—at least one hundred words for "tired." Luckily, moms have each other with whom to share woes, battle stories, secrets, and the little sustaining daily triumphs, too.

Rise above the crap.

A mother's life is filled with it—literally for the first few years and figuratively thereafter. When it comes to sheer volume and variety, nobody is called upon to put up with as many piddling annoyances as Mom.

There's no snuggle like a mom snuggle.

Biologists posit that penguin parents and chicks identify each other by scent and unique vocalizations. Although no fieldwork has yet been conducted to support this related theory, we wouldn't be surprised if there's another way that chicks know their moms—the snuggle. Nothing else feels so warm, so right, so like love and home, as nestling into Mom.

She'd give the feathers off her back if she could.

Penguin moms (dads, too) feed their chicks right out of their mouths. While the corollary behavior isn't as direct (or slimy), their human compatriots in parenting certainly know all about giving their young the food off their plate. "You'd like more potatoes? Here, Honey, have mine." Call it the Mom Diet.

Call for time out.

Being a buddy to your kid is fun.
It's easy. It's also a recipe for disaster.
No decent parent takes pleasure in
disciplining her kids, but then again,
no one said this was an easy gig.
A game of pillow kickball in the living
room? That was probably Dad's idea.
The concept of time out? Almost
certainly invented by a mom.

You can't spell "momentum" without "mom."

Life is not a video game. You don't get extra lives. Moms know that the "power-ups" that really count are fresh air, exercise, nutritious meals, and a healthy home atmosphere. "Turn it off. Get off the couch. Go outside and play." Those are sage words of wisdom from the original "life coach"—Mom.

This too shall pass.

Sulky one minute, manic the next. Teenagers really do seem like a different species altogether. So, what's a mom to do? Well, not a lot, actually. The best moms seem to know instinctively that adolescence is a part of life's journey that requires a fair amount of self-navigation. Young adults are contemplating a vast, blank landscape known as the rest of their lives. Let them explore. Let them try on different personalities and decide for themselves who they want to be.

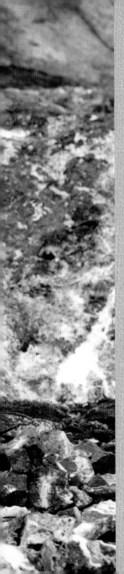

At your own peril

We all know what a mother's love is, right? Unconditional. Nurturing. Warm and fuzzy. Know what else it is? Fierce. Agatha Christie once wrote, "A mother's love for her child is like nothing else in the world. It knows no law, no pity. It dares all things and crushes down remorselessly all that stands in its path." Bam. How's that for warm and fuzzy?

When life's not fair, she'll be there.

Kids can be cruel. Good guys don't always finish first. Dark clouds are not contractually obligated to have silver linings. No one likes to be the bearer of bad news or the deliverer of harsh realities—especially to wide-eyed kids who believe in goodness and magic. The parceling out of difficult truths is best done by empathetic professionals. That means moms. No one can match them when it comes to weaving the tough stuff in among the goodness and magic (and, yes, life holds plenty of that, too).

You are being watched.

Sure there are days (years, even) when moms would swear kids pay no attention to what they say or do. The truth is they are always observing—and subconsciously filing away what they see and hear.

Influences are everywhere. Decent role models are not. Let's face it, no "real housewives" of anywhere are going to teach kids the proper way to behave, to carry themselves, and to mature. Only real moms can do that.

One clear moment

Ask a hundred mothers what gift they'd most like to receive. A blue-boxed bauble from Tiffany? A kitchen remodel? A couch sans Magic Marker hieroglyphs? All would finish a distant second to that one thing most precious and elusive to moms— time. Time to reset. Time to reflect. Time to reacquaint with that person she used to know so well—herself.

A mom for all seasons

It's not hard to be happy in good times. And it's natural to be down in the bad. What really distinguishes a person is how she carries herself on a gray day— when the sun doesn't shine, no fresh breeze blows, and the world seems to wallow in blah. Who always manages to tease beams of brightness out of a gray day? Indispensible, incandescent, effervescent Mom.

Full immersion

A mother's love doesn't materialize out of the blue at the moment of delivery. It isn't born at that first instance of eye-to-eye, but long, long before. It begins as a love borne of possibility. Then anticipation. A mother's love grows as her baby grows inside, building in intensity, so when the babe finally does arrive, she finds herself positively immersed in the stuff. The transition (from shell to nest, from womb to cradling arms) isn't easy, but the saturation of a mother's love makes it the most natural thing in the world.

House Beautiful can wait

To be a mother is to master the art of prioritization. For most moms, a typical day's to-do list goes something like this: Wake kids (or be awakened by small kids), feed kids, dress kids, drive kids, pick up after kids, worry about kids, drive kids some more, feed kids, clean kids, put kids to bed, crash . . . and repeat. So, yes, if the home front gets to looking a little rough by the end of the week, so be it. This is not a magazine shoot. This is real life.

Coping secrets of the successful mom

When behavior is relentlessly bad, when patience wears thin and energy wears out, experienced moms know that there's a reward waiting at the end of the day. (And not just the one served in a tall-stemmed glass.) When the day is done, she can tiptoe into the bedroom and see her "little angels" quietly, blissfully sleeping. It's even better than wine for forgetting and forgiving the battles of the day.

Here's the thing about dirt . . . it washes away.

Crib is swapped for big-boy bed seemingly overnight. Toddling becomes tearing around the house in a flash. Diapers to Pull-Ups to big-girl panties. Stroller to tricycle to scooter to bike. Childhood speeds. Adolescence is a blur. From a rearview perspective, the years we have with our children are fleeting and golden. Yes, they come home muddy once in a while. Someday—and it won't be long—they won't be coming home at all. Would any mother trade the mess for the memories?

Let them go.

It's a mom's job to be ever watchful, fiercely protective, and deeply engaged in her children's lives. It's also a mom's job to let go—to send them into the big scary world, whether that means walking away without looking back on the first day of kindergarten or nudging them gently out of the nest as young adults. Self-reliance and a sense of adventure are two of the best gifts moms can give.

Always enough

Whether it's a houseful of her own kids or someone else's, and whether they deserve it or not, there is always enough love to go around. No matter how weary, how frazzled, how worried she may be, the reservoir of love that is Mother never gets depleted. How do moms do it?

There's everyone else, then there's Mom.

The whole world over, my whole life through, there'll never be anyone who means so much to me as my unmatchable, unforgettable, unflappable mom.

Image key

Front Cover
Chinstrap penguins
Pygoscelis antarctica
Though they can occur all around Antarctica, chinstrap breeding populations are concentrated on the Antarctic Peninsula where an estimated 99% of the world's population occurs.

Page vi
Chinstrap penguins
Half Moon Island, South Shetland Islands
Always clamoring to be fed, chinstrap chicks grow rapidly on a diet of regurgitated krill. They get fed twice daily for the first two weeks, then less regularly as they get larger.

Page 3
Chinstrap penguins
Half Moon Island, South Shetland Islands
Pairs of chicks are common, but if the clutch is reduced to one chick, the surviving bird grows much faster.

Page 4
Adélie penguins
Pygoscelis adelie
Antarctic Peninsula
When there are few adults around for protection, older Adélie chicks gather together in clusters called crèches.

Page 7
Emperor penguins
Aptenodytes fosteri
Amery Ice Shelf
Emperor penguin chicks begin to lose their downy feathers (fledging) in November and December when they are between 100 and 150 days old.

Page 8
Adélie penguins
Antarctic Peninsula
When it is warm, the well-insulated Adélie penguins will hold their flippers akimbo for maximum cooling effect from the blood vessels that are close to the skin in the less densely feathered areas of their bodies.

Page 10
Chinstrap penguins
Half Moon Island, South Shetland Islands
With global warming, the Antarctic Peninsula is often above freezing and the rookeries become mud puddles when it rains, or the snow melts.

Page 12
Chinstrap penguins
Half Moon Island, South Shetland Islands
Chinstraps occupy the highest rocky points suitable for nesting, as these are the first to become snow free and in turn offer the longest potential breeding period.

Page 14
Adélie penguins
Cape Denison, Commonwealth Bay
Adélie chicks grow rapidly and
within weeks they are too large
to shelter under the parent in a
rocky nest. Up until this point the
parents take turns at guarding their
offspring.

Page 16
Rockhopper penguins
Eudyptes chrysocome
New Island, Falkland Islands
Rockhopper penguin adults
identify themselves to their mates
minding the nest with a series of
vocalizations each time one of them
returns from feeding.

Page 19
Gentoo penguins
Pygoscelis papua
Brown Bluff, Antarctic Peninsula
Gentoos nest on rocky coastal
beaches and the colonies become
whitewashed with acrid-smelling
guano. Its color is an indication of
their diet. White suggests a diet
predominantly of fish.

Page 21
Adélie penguins
Antarctic Peninsula
For the first three weeks after the
chicks hatch, Adélie parents take
daylong turns at minding their
offspring.

Page 22
Chinstrap penguins
Antarctic Peninsula
Regurgitated shrimplike crustacea,
Antarctic krill, is fed to the chicks in
multiple extended feeding sessions
when the adult returns from
foraging.

Page 25
Adélie penguins
Cape Denison, Commonwealth Bay
The dense down plumage Adélie
chicks acquire by three weeks of age
is just one of the many adaptations
that enable them to survive in
extreme conditions.

Page 27
King penguins
South Georgia
King penguin chicks grow to a very
large size and look so different
from their parents that at first early
explorers thought they were a
different species.

Page 29
Emperor penguins
Amery Ice Shelf
Fledging emperor penguin chicks
gain their juvenile plumage in
November and December, by which
time they are ready to go to sea to
begin foraging for themselves.

Page 30
Gentoo penguins
Antarctic Peninsula
A gentoo breeding pair takes turns at incubating their eggs for an average of 35 days before hatching occurs.

Page 33 and Back Cover
King penguins
Apetendoytes patagonica
South Georgia
King penguins can raise only one chick at a time because a pair takes turns at balancing a single egg on their feet during the incubation phase. The resulting chick is reared over such an extended time that a pair can breed only twice every three years.

Page 34
Emperor penguins
Amery Ice Shelf
Emperor penguins are the largest and most majestic of all the penguin species. Adults measure between 44 and 52 inches in height (110 and 130 cm), and their fledglings are bigger than the adults of all other penguin species, barring the king penguin.

Page 37
Chinstrap penguins
Half Moon Island, South Shetland Islands
Penguins never really sleep soundly for fear of predation, but they often nap standing up for minutes at a time, any time of day or night.

Page 38
Adélie penguins
Antarctic Peninsula
Red guano covering the colony indicates the Adélies have been feeding predominantly on Antarctic krill.

Page 41
Gentoo penguins
Antarctic Peninsula
On the Antarctic Peninsula in December, breeding gentoos begin laying two similarly sized eggs within a three-day period.

Page 42
Gentoo penguins
Brown Bluff, Antarctic Peninsula
Gentoos make stone nests to help keep eggs and chicks above meltwater should the temperature rise sufficiently to produce rain or snow melt.

Page 44
Gentoo penguins
Antarctic Peninsula
For protection gentoo chicks gather in crèches at four to five weeks of age, allowing both parents to go to sea to feed.

Page 46
Adélie penguins
Antarctic Peninsula
Without a good waterproof coating on their downy feathers, Adélie penguin chicks are vulnerable to rain and cold.

Page 53
Adélie penguins
Antarctic Peninsula
Adélie penguin adults and their chicks have feathers to the very tip of their bills, one of the many adaptations giving them the ability to survive the extreme conditions.

Page 48
Emperor penguins
Antarctic Peninsula
Emperor penguin chicks are often small when they first have to go to sea to fend for themselves. However, this occurs at the beginning of summer when the food supply is plentiful, so they are able to survive.

Page 51
Emperor penguins
Amery Ice Shelf
In October and November, emperor chicks move about in groups. They huddle when the weather is bad, waiting for their parents, both of which go to sea to forage. As summer approaches, the distance to the feeding grounds decreases and the parents can return daily or every other day to feed their chick. Once nearby, they identify each other with a series of trilling calls.

About the Authors

Jonathan Chester is a veteran polar photographer. The photographs in this book are from his many Antarctic expeditions. Patrick Regan has written lots of books—some with penguins, some without. You can learn more about Jonathan and Patrick and their books at extremeimages.com and patrickreganbooks.com.

Chester and Regan previously collaborated on the books *Flipping Brilliant: A Penguin's Guide to a Happy Life, To Love Is to Fly,* and *Stay Cool: A Polar Bear's Guide to Life.*

This book is dedicated with great love and thanks to our own unflappable moms: Thyra Yvette Chester and Patty Regan.

—JC & PR